Eileen Chong

Dark Matter

UNIVERSITY OF CANBERRA

Dark Matter
Second Edition
IPSI with Recent Work Press
Canberra, Australia
Copyright © Eileen Chong, 2018

ISBN: 978-0-6489367-1-8 (paperback)

First published 2018, this edition, 2020
International Poetry Studies Institute
Faculty of Arts and Design
University of Canberra
Canberra, Australia
ipsi.org.au

All rights reserved. This book is copyright. Except for private study, research, criticism or reviews as permitted under the Copyright Act, no part of this book may be reproduced, stored in a retrieval system, or transmitted in any form by any means without prior written permission. Enquiries should be addressed to the publisher.

Design by Caren Florance

Eileen Chong

Dark Matter

IPSI CHAPBOOK 12

University of Canberra
International Poetry Studies Institute
Series Editor: Paul Munden

For Colin Cassidy

The cosmos is within us.
We are made of star stuff.

Carl Sagan

Contents

Cosmos	1
Dark Matter	2
Paper Boats	3
Seeking Heaven	4
Water / Cycle	5
A Thousand Blooms	6
Peaches	7
Emilia	8
Woman, Crying	9
Guts	10
Victory	11
Coins	12
Forgetting	13
Green Grief	14
My Mother Talks in Numbers	15
My Mother, Painting	16
Windows, Singapore	17
Dog Meals	18
Rainbow	19
Spring Festival	20
Notes	23

Cosmos

The Museum of Modern Art, Tokyo

This tea bowl, built by hand.
Asymmetrical and balanced.

Crushed stone from the Kamo.
Chojiro's red and black glazes.

The hollow ring of low-fired clay.
What matters is not the vessel.

We are all perfectly imperfect—
each hairline crack a vein on the map.

Dark Matter

> I gave up colour.
>
> *Hu Liu, on 'Grass'*

Dark matter. Burnt wood, ground to
a fine powder, mixed with water.
Compressed into bricks. Build this.

What we know is rarely black and white.
Dense, layered, opaque. Graphite.
In these strokes: time rendered visible.

The sea: ink and water on paper.
Shadows, tidal pools, the surge.
In a wall of mirrors, waves break

open unto themselves. Fingermarks
in clay. Trees coaxed into characters.
Light scattered, spinning on plaster.

Paper Boats

after Bing Xin

They say the first year is for paper
—I have saved you all my poems.

The moon is full behind the clouds.
I fold each sheet along unseen lines.

Lengthwise, in half; here, a triangle.
Push, like this, and open it, carefully.

Little boats, with a shelter on each end.
What will stop them from breaking on rocks?

At the water, I bend and lower each craft into
the stream. The current takes hold immediately.

The grass is flattened where I have knelt.
Along the bank, the earth has turned into mud.

I follow each white fragment as it floats
downriver. Words are heavy. Paper boats sink.

Seeking Heaven

> And in the hollow of my ink-stained palms
> swallows will make their nest.
>
> 'Reborn', Forugh Farrokhzad
translated from the Farsi
by Sholeh Wolpé

This grass bed,
ringed by tussocks.
The snowmelt is receding.

Sweep of pebbles:
a broken wave,
milk-heavy breast.

A line of buried stones
punctuates the spine.
Dark mane, unbound.

Hands weighted
and open on emptied
sky-blue cloth, over full belly.

Press one ear to the ground—
storks cannot sing; can only clatter.

Water / Cycle

All I want
is to be the river though I return
again and again to the clouds.

> 'Time to be the fine line of light',
> Carrie Fountain

I hover above the river in an aeroplane,
marveling at how it looks like a photograph
or a map I once drew at school. It is an old river—
its banks are wide; its path is sinuous, meandering.

Here, an ox-bow lake, formed when the current
grew too slow to carry any more silt. *Billabong.*
That afternoon, children from the next class
emerged with new names on their lips: *cumulus,*

cirrus, cumulonimbus. I saw their diagrams: closed
systems. Moisture evaporates from the ocean
into the air and condenses into clouds; rain falls
over the land. Arrows cycle from river, to sea,

into cloud, back to river. They are too young to know—
Not all clouds bring rain. Not all rivers join the sea.

A Thousand Blooms

> Look here, children—
> There, by your feet,
> A tiny yellow flower!
>
> 'Don't Trample This Flower', Bing Xin,
> translated from the Chinese by Herbert Batt
> and Sheldon Zitner

Little ones, let's put pencil to paper—
draw the backyard rooster, sketch your loyal dog:
one to announce daybreak, the other to watch all night.

Let's shape their bodies with our hands.
Let's gouge out cavities with our fingers.
We are a hundred lidless eyes.

You there, go out into the desert.
Come back when you've stopped weeping.
Who shall we drown in glass today?
Who will withstand the flames?

The blue-and-white vases are broken.
They made us walk across the shards.
Our cut feet are a thousand crimson blooms.
It's certain death for flowers without roots.

Peaches

What things are steadfast? Not the birds.
'We Manage Most When We Manage Small',
Linda Gregg

For days now I have wandered, every step
sunk into sand. Even the air is heavy. The light
colours green through the leaves, opaque where
shadows are cast. I count and weigh the pebbles

in my pockets. *What is it? What is it?* The birds
sing out from the trees. Five, six, seven stones—
they lit the candles. She blew them out, exhaling.
Sweet buns filled with lotus paste, moulded

into peaches: like longevity, ripe and heavy,
hanging from a low branch. You draw a blind
fingertip across the top of my lip to feel each
invisible hair. Under this skin: only bruised flesh.

Emilia

The babies made me invincible.
'Invincible', Maggie Smith

Her eyes (still grey, blue, and green) search
mine out. I meet her gaze, then hold her.

She bobs her head at me, and I lower mine
in return. Our foreheads meet and cleave.

I tilt her backwards, my hand cradling her neck,
then lift her towards me, and tilt her again.

She clings to me—freedom and safety,
safety and freedom. It is a game she knows,

and she smiles, and smiles. Her laughter,
a talisman; her eyes, a ward. She sees me,

and so I exist. I am here, and I suffer.
Soon she will go, and my love with her.

I wake to the smell of milk. The hungry
mouth. The animal grip of her clenched fists.

Woman, Crying

So close to the end of my childbearing life
without children

'The Girl', Marie Howe

I sat in the café while your friend railed at me
—*If you knew you were going to leave why did you try,
and keep try*ing—he meant for children, of course,

though we did not have them in the end.
Which comes first, blame or consequence?
I sat there, crying, while waitresses tiptoed

around me. One slipped me a napkin. I'd like
to go back. I'd like to have stood up, thrown water
in his face, smashed the plates onto the ground,

and yelled *It's none of your fucking business!* I'd like
to have been the woman who made a scene. Instead,
I sat there and wept, unable to find the words

to say how I'd wanted to bear your children,
how much I loved you, and when each of them
failed to draw breath, how parts of me died, too.

Guts

> ... I would say
> I love it, what's in my body,
> but I want you to love it too.
>
> *'Answer 3', Devin Kelly*

I was searching for the poet when I found
the man who'd opened fire in a church in Texas.

He shot and killed twenty-six people that day—
mothers, fathers, sons, and daughters. A woman
with a baby inside her who would never enter the world

whole. I began again. I found the poet and his words
but now with the weight of all those who'd died.

I think about how our bodies lay all those years
in the same bed, not touching. How I wanted him
to want me. Now I see what he couldn't bear

to touch was himself. How he couldn't look me
in the eye and not see his body like a mirror.

Still, my body was blood and guts and heart. How
I would sigh if his skin brushed mine in the dark. And
how, if he'd pressed against me, I'd have crumbled into dust.

Victory

This is the only language
men like them can speak.
You either belong to them,
or must belong to another.

Men like them will speak;
they drip with honeyed words.
Perhaps you belong to another.
You exist as a coveted trophy.

They drip with honey, words that
spin dreams, make promises.
You covet being the trophy:
a prize so wanton, so wanted.

Spin your dreams, break promises.
You now belong to them.
Their prize, once won, is unwanted.
Victory is their singular language.

Coins

after Carol Ann Duffy's 'Hour'

This evening, in the train station,
I ascended, you descended—
our eyes met, then I turned away.
My husband was behind me, and
you went home, to your wife and child.

It's hard to believe I once felt
hunger for you, that a stolen
glance would carry meanings (I know
now) were empty. No treasure there—
just these coins, dropped, buried in mud.

Forgetting

I sing to comfort myself.
The cats know why we sleep
all day. The winds have arrived
with autumn; mornings dawn crisp.

I tell everyone I have forgotten—
with each retelling, memory etches
a deeper groove. I have a home
to clean, and men's shirts to iron.

I know what I must do
to get dinner on the table.
I have everything I need:
the sharpened knife awaits.

Green Grief

I heard about your wedding in a Catholic church so much food and wine live jazz band how you'd lost all that weight everyone so happy. Revenge fantasies: you fell off a cliff got run over by a truck you were buried up to your neck drizzled with honey and left for the ants your plane went down over the Pacific you had a heart attack you were shot in the eye. You see, poets have this thing for truth. The memory of crying so hard I threw up but in the shower so you wouldn't hear though there was no door on the bathroom. My therapist says I had a choice I probably was the problem I couldn't be the woman who would sit down and shut up or stand in a cupboard all day waiting until you got home and unlocked it. In my dream you were in my house and my friend who is also a poet said I have to tell you to vacate the premises because you would never ever acknowledge what you did to me. Larkin said *Last year is dead* and to *Begin afresh, afresh, afresh*. Repetition here is key.

My Mother Talks in Numbers

What is home?
Forty years of morning, noon, and night.

Tell me about your childhood.
Thirty-seven mouths open under a tin roof.

What is happiness?
Eighteen in my sailor suit, spray from the waterfall—

Why did you marry?
Five years of coins.

How many tears?
One thousand, eight hundred, and ninety-eight pearls.

Do you love your mother?
Two hands, ten fingers, six children.

How many miles have you come?
Sixty-four thousand and twenty-five gull-wings.

Do you love me?
The rain falling, falling, over thirteen thousand dawns.

My Mother, Painting

My mother sends me an image
of her painting of the week. I reply:
I think the original will be hard to beat.

She spends hours copying masterpieces:
Hopper's lighthouse, Smithson's spiral,
Da Vinci's Mona Lisa. When I got married,

she gave us a likeness of me, aged three,
sitting along the five-foot-way outside
our shophouse on Victoria Street.

She didn't like it. *I couldn't get your face right.*
There's only a blur of beige with pale lips
and dark eyes. My feet are suspended;

I was swinging my legs. She's painted in
the motorbike belonging to the man
who welded metal bars. Fire sparking

across the pavement; the iron-rich stench
of hot steel. Inside the office, someone
strokes me in the darkness when I hide

under the table. The orange lamps of the altar
burn like witnesses; incense blankets
the air. A finger is pressed across my lips.

Later, in the kitchen, I suck on a lemon lolly
and wonder when I will get more. Bruises
on my thighs. Take up the brush—Prussian

blue, vermillion red. Yet the paint has dried;
the painting is framed. My mother cannot
craft in art what she never saw in life.

Windows, Singapore

Bleary-eyed in the dark—these
are our suburban compatriots.
It's an hour on the bus to school.

I sit next to a boy whom I never
speak to outside of our journeys.
Today he is giving me a blow-

by-blow account of a movie he watched
last night. He always wakes me up before
our stop. He doesn't laugh when my head

sometimes hits the glass. I have a boyfriend
who lives in the city. His father drives him
every morning on the way to work as Director

of Singapore Telecommunications. On some days,
my boyfriend takes the bus home with me
so we can lock ourselves in my bedroom.

Air-conditioner blasting—sweat-free make-out sessions
on long afternoons. He is always invited to stay to dinner.
Afterwards, he takes a taxi home and pays for it with money

his grandfather gives him because my home is so far away
and it's too dark to walk down the streets of fenced-in houses
where he lives. It's quiet there and people mind their own
    business.

Where I live: strip lights along corridors, footsteps on the ceiling.
Eyes line uncountable windows. I hear my neighbour coughing.
The endless shuffle of mahjong tiles like dull prayers in the night.

Dog Meals

The dead women always fed me.
In their kitchens, water ran from brass taps,
next to the thick wooden chopping blocks
where the chinese cleavers lay glistening—

bowls of sliced pork belly braised in soy,
trembling with fat; plates of wok-seared rice
dry-fried to a near-crisp with onion and garlic;
cabbage, black fungus and beancurd skins

stewed with glass noodles and dried shrimp.
I have eaten of these willingly. The last woman
to die consumed three whole meals of the new
dog year before she lay her head down in the dark,

never to wake again to brew strong coffee
with condensed milk, to spread kaya on toast,
to crack open soft-boiled eggs. Nothing left but
a procession of black ants crawling across the counter.

Rainbow

after Elizabeth Bishop's 'The Fish'

On the first day, we ate the trout
with its skin on. Scales in my teeth.
You said: let the knife do the work.
*

The second day, I laid the fish out
onto its side; I pinched its edge and slid
the blade clean between fat and muscle.
*

Not all rainbow: here, tender orange,
there, rusted brown, the underside
gelatinous and white. Then the bones.
*

Over lunch, the man and the woman
carved fillets from each other
one word at a time.
*

The cat licks remnants of flesh
from flayed skin. Its tongue:
red, methodical, and barbed.
*

Nothing left for the third day
save the offcuts. Cubes of cured
trout layered on pickles and rice.
*

How to multiply one fish into many—
my mother ties an unseen knot. The string
is invisible, but the hooked fish still pulls.

Spring Festival

The feeling begins in the stomach:
a stone pit swallowed by accident,
indigestible as homesickness.

My husband reminds me I write poems
in threes: three lines, three pathways.
One for the old life, one for the new

days to come, and one for the hours
I do not notice as they pass. I bought
twelve mandarin oranges on the eve

of the new year. On the first day
we took them to my parents' home.
My father gave me oranges and grapefruit

in return: I did not know why, or what
to do with them. On the second day,
I woke to the sun's rays across my face.

In the kitchen, my husband sliced
the fruit and squeezed each half.
He saved the pulp, added grated ginger,

then handed me a glass of bright juice.
It was sweet, and cold, and it filled me;
I consume his love and care with greed.

Once, I watched a video of forty men
crouched around a concrete tank
brimming with water, holding a frame

larger than our apartment. To the count
of one voice, they hoist, dip, and lift;
they coax the white pulp to flow and settle

across a tightly stretched cloth mesh.
They move through a complex dance,
forearms sunk in liquid, feet marching

from tank to drying rack, and back again.
On the morning news, blonde children
speak Mandarin and write the character

for prosperity repeatedly, perfectly.
I reach for paper and ink, I mark this page;
I seek an address, I want to be delivered home.

Notes

'Cosmos' was inspired by a visit to the exhibition *The Cosmos in a Tea Bowl: Transmitting A Secret Art Across Generations of the Raku Family*, 14 March–21 May 2017, at the National Museum of Modern Art, Tokyo, Japan.

'Dark Matter' was inspired by a visit to the exhibition *The Dark Matters*, 8 March–30 July 2017, at the White Rabbit Gallery, NSW, Australia.

'Seeking Heaven' was commissioned by *Peril Magazine* as part of a collaborative project with the art exhibition *Hyphenated*, 22 March–21 April 2018, at The Substation, VIC, Australia. It was written in response to the artwork of Sofi Basseghi, 'Finding Paradise'.

'A Thousand Blooms' was commissioned by *Peril Magazine* as part of a collaborative project with the art exhibition *Hyphenated*, 22 March–21 April 2018, at The Substation, VIC, Australia. It was written in response to the artwork of Vipoo Srivilasa, 'Superhero'.

'Woman, Crying' was commissioned by *The Lifted Brow* for the June 2018 issue.

'Green Grief' was commissioned by *Spineless Wonders* for its 'Time' anthology (2017), edited by Cassandra Atherton, and derives its title and quoted lines from Philip Larkin's 'The Trees'.

'My Mother, Painting' was commissioned by *The Lifted Brow* for the June 2018 issue.

'Dog Meals' was published in a special English-language section with the theme of 'Food', in *Voice and Verse Magazine*, Issue 41, May 2018.

'Rainbow' was published in *The Margins*, the online poetry journal of the Asian American Writers' Workshop, 31 July 2018.

Eileen Chong is a Sydney poet who was born in Singapore. She is the author of six books, the most recent being *Rainforest*, from Pitt Street Poetry. Individual poems of hers have shortlisted for the Newcastle Poetry Prize, twice for the Peter Porter Poetry Prize, and longlisted three times for the University of Canberra Vice-Chancellor's International Poetry Prize. Her books have been shortlisted for the Anne Elder Award, the Victorian Premier's Literary Award, and twice for the Prime Minister's Literary Awards.

www.eileenchong.com.au

IPSI: International Poetry Studies Institute

The International Poetry Studies Institute (IPSI) is part of the Centre for Creative and Cultural Research, Faculty of Arts and Design, University of Canberra. IPSI conducts research related to poetry, and publishes and promulgates the outcomes of this research internationally. The institute also publishes poetry and interviews with poets, as well as related material, from around the world. Publication of such material takes place in IPSI's online journal *Axon: Creative Explorations* (www.axonjournal.com.au) and through other publishing vehicles, such as Axon Elements. IPSI's goals include working – collaboratively, where possible – for the appreciation and understanding of poetry, poetic language and the cultural and social significance of poetry. The institute also organises symposia, seminars, readings and other poetry-related activities and events.

IPSI Chapbook Series

The IPSI Chapbook Series publishes new work by leading poets from Australia and beyond, in limited editions. The chapbooks feature extended selections beyond the scope of most journals, highlighting innovative work by poets both new and well established, ahead of publication in book form. The series is linked to an international program of poets in residence at the University of Canberra. Series Editor: Paul Munden.

CCCR: Centre for Creative & Cultural Research

The Centre for Creative and Cultural Research (CCCR) is IPSI's umbrella organisation and brings together staff, adjuncts, research students and visiting fellows who work on key challenges within the cultural sector and creative field. A central feature of its research concerns the effects of digitisation and globalisation on cultural producers, whether individuals, communities or organisations.

www.ingramcontent.com/pod-product-compliance
Lightning Source LLC
Chambersburg PA
CBHW070714020526
44107CB00078B/2578